★★★★★

MLB TEAMS

ATHLETICS

KENNY ABDO

Fly!
An Imprint of Abdo Zoom
abdobooks.com

abdobooks.com

Published by Abdo Zoom, a division of ABDO, P.O. Box 398166, Minneapolis, Minnesota 55439.

Printed in the United States of America, North Mankato, Minnesota.
102025
012026

THIS BOOK CONTAINS RECYCLED MATERIALS

Photo Credits: Alamy, AP Images, Getty Images, Shutterstock
Production Contributors: Kenny Abdo, Jennie Forsberg, Grace Hansen
Design Contributors: Candice Keimig, Neil Klinepier

Library of Congress Control Number: 2025936757

Publisher's Cataloging-in-Publication Data

Names: Abdo, Kenny, author.
Title: Athletics / by Kenny Abdo
Description: Minneapolis, Minnesota : Abdo Zoom, 2026 | Series: MLB teams | Includes online resources and index.
Identifiers: ISBN 9798384940098 (lib. bdg.) | ISBN 9798384940852 (ebook) | ISBN 9798384941231 (read-to-me ebook)
Subjects: LCSH: Athletics (Baseball team)--Juvenile literature. | Baseball teams--Juvenile literature. | Professional sports--Juvenile literature. | Sports franchises--Juvenile literature. | Major League Baseball (Organization)--Juvenile literature.
Classification: DDC 796.357--dc23

Table of CONTENTS

ATHLETICS

Whether in Philadelphia, Oakland, or on the dazzling Las Vegas Strip, the Athletics bring the heat. No matter the city, the team always shines in green and gold!

A's
Athletics

With exciting World Series wins and fresh ideas like the **Moneyball** system, the Athletics have earned straight A's for more than just their baseball skills!

OAKLAND
A's
WORLD CHA
IONS

BATTER UP!

The Athletics were founded in Philadelphia, Pennsylvania, in 1901 as one of the original **American League** (**AL**) teams. The A's had a strong start, winning their first World Series title in 1910!

Legendary **General Manager (GM)** Connie Mack led the Athletics in the team's early decades. Under his leadership, the A's won five World Series titles by 1930. Many fans still consider this **era** the A's golden years.

The A's moved to Kansas City, Missouri, in 1955. Success in their new city was hard to find. During their 13 seasons there, the team never reached the World Series. It was a difficult stretch for both the team and its loyal fans.

GRAND SLAMS

The A's found a new home in Oakland in 1968. The California sun may have been just what the team needed. From 1972 to 1974, the A's won three straight World Series titles. This incredible **era** introduced fans to legends like Reggie Jackson and Rollie Fingers.

ST. LOUIS CARDINALS
OAKLAND ATHLETICS
NEW YORK YANKEES
MILWAUKEE BREWERS
Kansas City ROYALS
CHICAGO
BOSTON RED SOX
BALTIMORE ORIOLES
ATLANTA BRAVES
CHICAGO CUBS
Los Angeles DODGERS
OAKLAND
1974 WORLD

SAN FRANCISCO GIANTS
1989 National League Champions
GIANTS
'89 World Series
Athletics
BATTLE of the BAY

In 1989, the A's faced the San Francisco Giants in the World Series known as the "Battle of the Bay." The Loma Prieta earthquake struck just before Game 3, delaying the series for ten days. The A's would go on to **sweep** the Giants in four games! A's Pitcher Dave Stewart was named series MVP.

BRAD PITT
MONEYBALL
JONAH HILL PHILIP SEYMOUR HOFFMAN
BASED ON A TRUE STORY
COLUMBIA PICTURES PRESENTS A SCOTT RUDIN/MICHAEL DE LUCA/RACHAEL HOROVITZ PRODUCTION A FILM BY BENNETT MILLER
"MONEYBALL" MUSIC BY MYCHAEL DANNA COSTUME DESIGNER KASIA WALICKA MAIMONE EDITED BY CHRISTOPHER TELLEFSEN, A.C.E. PRODUCTION DESIGNER JESS GONCHOR DIRECTOR OF PHOTOGRAPHY WALLY PFISTER, ASC
EXECUTIVE PRODUCERS SCOTT RUDIN ANDREW KARSCH SIDNEY KIMMEL MARK BAKSHI BASED ON THE BOOK BY MICHAEL LEWIS STORY BY STAN CHERVIN SCREENPLAY BY STEVEN ZAILLIAN AND AARON SORKIN
PRODUCED BY MICHAEL DE LUCA RACHAEL HOROVITZ BRAD PITT
THIS FALL
DIRECTED BY BENNETT MILLER
THIS FILM IS NOT YET RATED. FOR FUTURE INFO GO TO FILMRATINGS.COM
Moneyball-Movie.com
Soundtrack on Madison Gate Records
SONY
COLUMBIA PICTURES

By 2002, the A's had shaken things up with their new **Moneyball** system. Led by **GM** Billy Beane, the team won 103 games and set an **AL record** with a 20-game winning streak. Other teams started to notice, and so did Hollywood. The film *Moneyball*, starring Brad Pitt as Beane, was released in 2011.

THANK YO
SO LONG

In 2023, the A's announced their plan to move to Las Vegas. They ended that season with a league-worst 50–112 **record**. The team played in Oakland through the 2024 season, winning their final home game. However, they lost their last game as the Oakland Athletics on the road.

In 2025, the A's began play in West Sacramento without a city name in their title. Brent Rooker put up a strong showing on the new but temporary turf. The **designated hitter** racked up 30 home runs and was a consistent source of runs and **RBIs**.

The Athletics and its fans look forward to a bright future and a new home in Las Vegas, Nevada.

HALL OF FAME

Reggie Jackson was a powerful hitter who played a key role in many historic A's moments. He helped the A's win three straight World Series titles from 1972 to 1974. Jackson was **inducted** into the Baseball Hall of Fame in 1993.

Rickey Henderson, known as the "Man of Steal," earned his nickname with the A's by often leading the league in stolen bases. In 1982, he set a major league **record** by stealing 130 bases in a single season. During his time in Oakland, Henderson stole 867 bases. He was named to the Baseball Hall of Fame in 2009.

A's
Oakland

Mark McGwire could punish a ball. He hit an impressive 363 home runs for the A's between 1986 and 1997. That is a team **record**. He would go on to hit 70 home runs in one season with the St. Louis Cardinals. McGwire later admitted to using performance-enhancing drugs. His supporters believe his talent and hard work outshine that cloud over his career.

GLOSSARY

American League (AL) – one of two 15-team leagues that make up MLB.

designated hitter – a baseball player who bats in place of another position player, most commonly the pitcher.

era – a period of time in history.

General Manager (GM) – the person who builds and runs the team by making trades, signing players, and making key decisions.

inducted – brought in as a member.

Moneyball – the use of metrics to identify undervalued players.

record – a team's season total of wins and losses; a top achievement by a player or team that no one has done before.

Runs Batted In (RBI) – a statistic that credits a batter for making a play that allows a run to be scored.

sweep – to win all games in a series.

ONLINE RESOURCES

Booklinks
NONFICTION NETWORK
FREE! ONLINE NONFICTION RESOURCES

To learn more about the Athletics, please visit **abdobooklinks.com** or scan this QR code. These links are routinely monitored and updated to provide the most current information available.

INDEX